ReMAKE ReSTYLE ReUSE

...to Fred (my love) + my two angels...

Sonia Lucano

Photography by Fred Lucano

ReMAKE ReSTYLE ReUSE

Easy Ways to Transform Everyday Basics into Inspired Design

Watson-Guptill Publications

New York

Glasses, plates, vases…
and other tableware

Blankets, sheets, towels…
and other household linens

Contents

Boxes, buckets, chests... and other containers

And still more...

Basic Techniques

How can you decorate your home with things that are different and original without spending a fortune?

The answer is simple: take something that costs next to nothing, add a dash of imagination, a bit of technique… and a little elbow grease. The materials are easy to find, and all the instructions you need are explained in this book. Select the designs you like and the materials you want to use, then create beautiful, unique items to decorate your home and express your style.

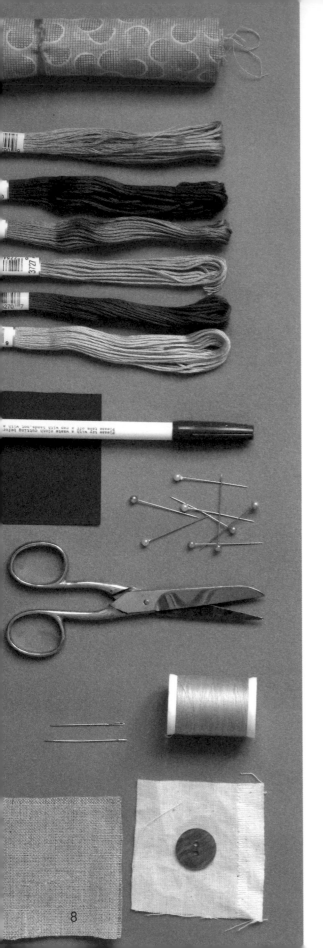

Embroidery

Materials
Cotton or linen fabric
Cotton embroidery thread (we used DMC embroidery floss)
Embroidery needle, scissors, and straight pins
Embroidery hoop
Dressmaker's carbon paper and tracing paper
Water-soluble fabric pen
Pencil

First, trace or photocopy the design you want to embroider. Lay your fabric on a flat surface and cover with a sheet of dressmaker's carbon paper, face down, where you want the design to be. Lay the traced or photocopied design on top of the carbon paper and go over all of the lines with a pencil, pressing hard.

You can also use stencils (for instructions on making these, see page 11). Just place the stencil directly on the fabric and trace the outline with a fabric pen.

Stretch your fabric in an embroidery hoop, centering the area you want to embroider in the hoop.

Separate the strands of embroidery floss, using 1 or 2 strands. (The more strands you use, the thicker the outline.) Thread the strand(s) onto your embroidery needle, and use the following stitches to create and embellish your design, as explained in each specific project.

Running stitch (3 stitches to ¾ in./2 cm)

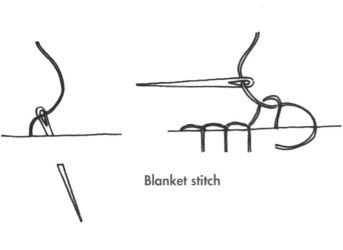

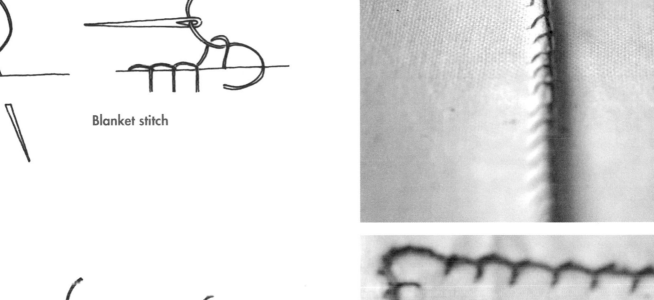

Blanket stitch

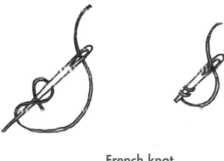

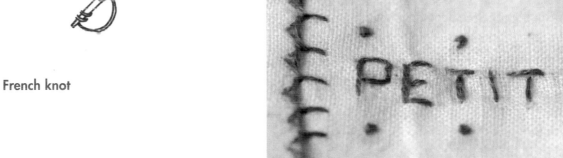

French knot

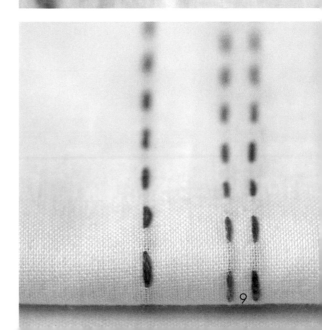

Stem stitch

Dyeing fabric

Dyeing by hand

Materials
Linen or cotton fabric (you may get paler colors using polyester/cotton blends)
Fabric dye (we used Dylon)
Large bowl
Salt (or other fixative recommended by the manufacturer)
Large wooden spoon
Rubber gloves

Wash the fabric to be dyed thoroughly and rinse well. Dissolve the dye in 2 cups (500 ml) hot water and pour into a large bowl. Dissolve the fixative in hot water and add to the bowl, then add enough cold water to completely cover the fabric. Work carefully; do not breathe in the dye or get it in your eyes or on your skin. Do not use dye around small children. Put the wet fabric into the dye, immersing it completely. Stir carefully for 5 to 10 minutes with a wooden spoon. Leave to soak for 1 hour, stirring occasionally. Finish by rinsing the fabric thoroughly until the water runs clear.

Machine dyeing

Materials
Linen or cotton fabric (you may get paler colors using polyester/cotton blends)
Fabric dye (we used Dylon)
Salt (or manufacturer's recommended fixative)
Rubber gloves

Prepare the fabric as above, washing and rinsing it thoroughly. Put the dye in the drum of the machine together with 1 pound (500g) of salt (or the manufacturer's recommended fixative). Add the wet fabric and run the machine through a complete cycle at 104°F (40°C), without adding any detergent. When the cycle is finished, add detergent and put the item through another wash cycle if this is recommended by the manufacturer. Remove the item when you're done. Then add washing detergent and run another cycle at 104°F (40°C) with the machine empty to clean it. There is no risk of damaging your washing machine by using it in this way. Dry the dyed fabric flat, away from direct heat or sunlight.

Using stencils and stamps

Stencils

Materials
Acetate or other clear plastic stencil film
Craft knife
Masking tape
Paintbrush or stencil brush
Stencil paint or crafter's acrylic paint

You can buy stencils ready made, or make your own.
Making your own is simple—just lay the acetate over
whatever designs or letters you want to use and trace them.
(See alphabet on pages 14–15.) You can use the designs
at actual size, or enlarge them on a photocopier first. Then
cut out the inside of each shape with a craft knife, and
remove the pieces. This will give you solid, reusable stencils.

To use, position the stencil on your surface and secure with
masking tape. The stenciling itself can be done with a paintbrush, or by tapping gently with a stencil brush for a lighter,
subtler finish.

Stamps

Materials
Rubber stamps
Ink pad or paint

Rubber stamps are readily available in stores—toy stores
and stationery stores usually have lots to choose from.
They are an easy and unusual way to decorate almost any
household item.

Make sure to choose ink or paint that is appropriate to the
material you are decorating, and follow the instructions on
pages 12–13.

Painting

There is a specific paint for every sort of material. Acrylic paint is used on wood and zinc; porcelain paint on dishes, tiles, and anything ceramic or porcelain; and fabric paint on textiles. Ink can be used on anything except zinc.

Painting on ceramic or porcelain

Materials
Porcelain paint(s)
Applicator tips or nozzles to fit the paint tubes
Natural turpentine (non-toxic)
Tracing paper
Soft pencil
Permanent felt-tip marker
Rubbing alcohol
Oven

Reproduce the design you've chosen using tracing paper and a soft pencil, as for painting with acrylic paint, but trace over the pencil lines with a permanent marker for a clearer outline of the design.

Painting on ceramics with a brush usually leaves brushstrokes, so it is better to use tips or nozzles especially made for that purpose. Use a fine nozzle for outlines and small details and a larger one to fill in large areas. Always work in a well-ventilated room and use a natural, non-toxic turpentine to clean the brushes.

When you're finished, let the paint dry for 30 minutes. Then place the object into a cold oven and heat to 300°F (150°C). Bake for 1 hour, then take it out of the oven and let it cool for 24 hours.

Finally, remove all remaining traces of the marker with cotton balls soaked in rubbing alcohol, rubbing gently and carefully around the painted area. Although your painted items may be dishwasher proof, knives may scratch the design, so we recommend using this technique on decorative items only.

Painting on wood or zinc

Materials
Acrylic paint(s)
Paintbrushes
Soft pencil
Tracing paper
Masking tape

Copy your design onto tracing paper using a soft pencil.
Turn the tracing paper over and trace over the lines thickly
with the pencil on the reverse side. Position the paper,
right side up, on the item to be painted and trace over the
lines once again, leaving the outline imprinted on the wood
or zinc.

Surround the design to be painted with masking tape so that
your outlines will be perfectly straight. You could also use
stencils (see page 11 for instructions on making stencils).
Paint the design, passing your brush over the masking tape,
then leave to dry before applying a second coat to ensure
a perfect finish with no brushstrokes. Wait until the paint is
completely dry before carefully pulling off the masking tape.

Painting on fabric

Materials
Fabric paint
Paintbrush
Tracing paper and dressmaker's carbon paper
Clean cloth
Iron

Copy your design onto fabric following the directions on
page 8. Once you have copied the design, apply the fabric
paint with a brush, tapping it gently and being careful not to
put too much paint on the brush. Let dry for at least 4 hours.
To set the paint, cover the design with a clean cloth and press
with a hot iron for 5 minutes, keeping the iron moving
constantly so you don't scorch the fabric.

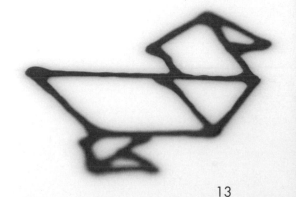

A B C D

E F G H

I J K

L M N

O P Q R
S T U V
W X
Y Z

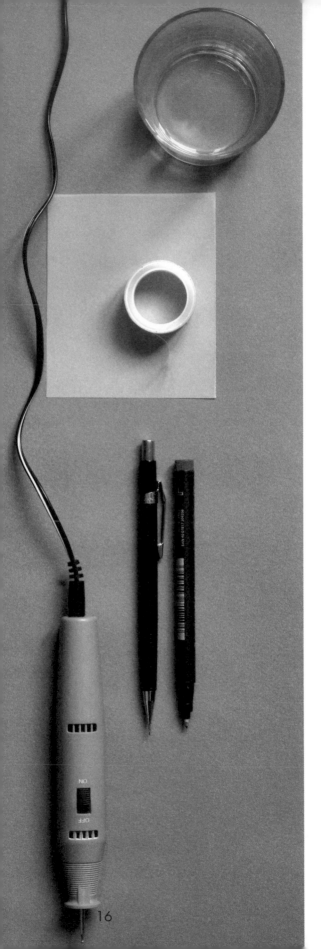

Engraving

Engraving glass

Materials
Glass engraving tool
Permanent felt-tip marker
Pencil, tracing paper, and white paper or photocopier
Masking tape
Soft brush such as camel's hair and a clean cloth
Rubbing alcohol
Safety glasses and a dust mask

Wash the glass item thoroughly in hot water and dry completely with a clean, dry cloth to avoid leaving any lint. Use a pencil and tracing paper or a photocopier to copy your design, then tape it inside the glass, where you want the engraving to be, with the right side of the design facing toward the glass. If you use tracing paper, tape a piece of white paper behind it so the design is easier to see. Use a marker to trace the design on the outside of the glass, then remove the paper.

Place the item on a plain, dark surface. Lighting is very important, and contrast is essential to see the work clearly. Look down vertically as you work, and steady the hand holding the engraving tool by supporting it at the same height as the design (for example, on a pile of books). Always wear protective glasses and a dust mask while engraving.

Gently clean the area with a soft brush as you work to wipe away the dust that is produced, then wipe with a clean cloth to prevent the tool from skidding. When you're finished, remove any remaining traces of the marker with a rubbing alcohol. To fill in solid areas, work slowly and patiently so the finished engraving is neat and even.

Engraving mirrors

For mirrors, trace the design with a soft pencil and then go over the lines thickly on the reverse of the tracing paper. Place the back of the tracing on the mirror and trace over the lines once again using a very soft pencil. This should transfer the design to the mirror. Draw over the lines again with the marker, then proceed as for glass, above.

Using decorative paper

Materials
Wallpaper or decorative paper
Craft knife
Ruler
Permanent spray adhesive
Clean cloth
Pin
Clear matte acrylic spray varnish
Ribbon or raffia
Clear-drying craft glue
Paintbrush
Dust mask

Cut the paper to the size of the item to be covered, using a craft knife and ruler to ensure straight edges. Lay the paper face down on a flat surface and coat the back with spray adhesive, wearing a dust mask while you spray. Glue the paper firmly onto your object, pressing firmly and smoothing with the cloth to get rid of any air bubbles. Pay particular attention to the corners for a good finish. If you notice any air bubbles that you missed after the glue has set, prick them carefully with a pin and press them flat. You can add ribbon or raffia using craft glue applied with a brush.

To protect the paper, and give it a durable, satin-like finish, cover with varnish. Once the paper is completely dry, spray the object evenly using a spray varnish, which is quicker than painting it on with a brush. Always wear a dust mask and make sure the room is properly ventilated when using spray adhesive or spray varnish.

Ruban de Soie
à broder

Glasses,
plates,
vases...
and other
tableware

Tea light holders
Instructions on pages 34–35

Personalized
wine glasses
Instructions on pages 36–37

Dotty bowls
Instructions on page 38

Vase cozy
Instructions on pages 38–39

Test-tube bud vases
Instructions on page 40

Autumn plates

Instructions on pages 42–43

Dandelion vase

Instructions on pages 44–45

Bouquet vase
Instructions on pages 46–47

Clover glasses
Instructions on pages 46–47

Tea light holders

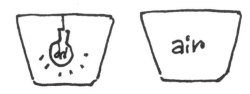

Materials
4 small glass tea light holders
Glass engraving tool
Pencil and tracing paper or photocopier
Scissors
Permanent felt-tip marker
Masking tape
Rubbing alcohol
Safety glasses
Dust mask

Use a photocopier or a pencil and tracing paper to copy the 4 designs on the left side of page 35. Cut the designs apart and tape one to the inside of each tea light holder, right side toward the glass, positioned where you want it to be. Trace over each design with marker on the outside of the glass, then remove the paper. Engrave the designs, wearing safety glasses and a dust mask and following the instructions on page 16. Finish by removing any traces of marker with rubbing alcohol.

Geometric carafe

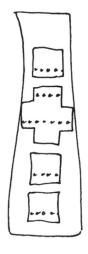

Materials
Glass carafe or pitcher with fairly straight sides
Glass engraving tool
Pencil and tracing paper or photocopier
Scissors
Permanent felt-tip marker
Masking tape
Rubbing alcohol
Safety glasses
Dust mask

Use a photocopier or a pencil and tracing paper to copy the design on right side of page 35. Tape it to the inside of the carafe, right side toward the glass. On the outside of the glass trace over the design with marker, then remove the paper. Engrave the design wearing safety glasses and a dust mask and following the instructions on page 16. Finish by removing any traces of marker with rubbing alcohol.

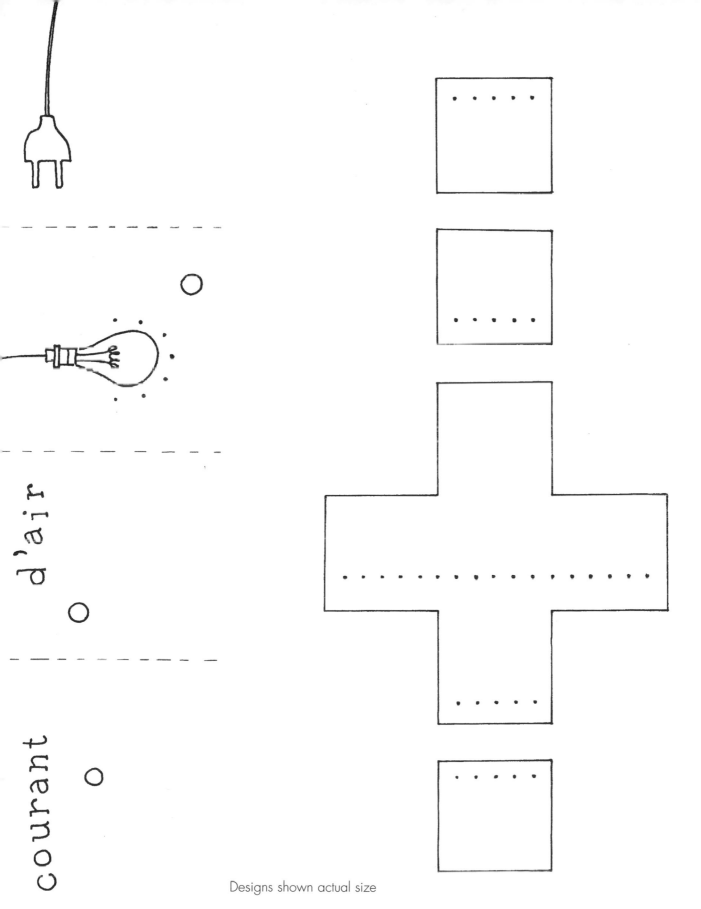

courant d'air

Designs shown actual size

Personalized wine glasses

Materials
Wine glasses (they don't have to match)
Glass engraving tool
Pencil and tracing paper or photocopier
Scissors
Permanent felt-tip marker
Masking tape
Rubbing alcohol
Safety glasses
Dust mask

Use a photocopier or a pencil and tracing paper to copy letters from the alphabets below and opposite to spell out a name, initials, or a favorite word.
Tape the name or word to the inside of each wine glass, right side toward the glass. On the outside of the glass trace over it with marker, then remove the paper. Engrave the letters wearing safety glasses and a dust mask and following the instructions on page 16. Finish by removing any traces of marker with solvent.

ABCDEFGHIJKLMN
OPQRSTUVWXYZ

abcdefghijklmn
opqrstuvwxyz

Letters shown actual size

$\mathcal{BA}$

$\mathcal{A}$ $\mathcal{B}$ $\mathcal{C}$ $\mathcal{D}$ $\mathcal{E}$ $\mathcal{F}$ $\mathcal{G}$

$\mathcal{H}$ $\mathcal{I}$ $\mathcal{J}$ $\mathcal{K}$ $\mathcal{L}$ $\mathcal{M}$ $\mathcal{N}$

$\mathcal{O}$ $\mathcal{P}$ $\mathcal{Q}$ $\mathcal{R}$ $\mathcal{S}$ $\mathcal{T}$ $\mathcal{U}$

$\mathcal{V}$ $\mathcal{W}$ $\mathcal{X}$ $\mathcal{Y}$ $\mathcal{Z}$

Letters shown actual size

Dotty bowls

Materials
Ceramic bowls and matching plates
Porcelain paint (we used purple)
Fine tip or nozzle for paint tube
Permanent felt-tip marker
¾-inch- (2-cm-) wide masking tape
Rubbing alcohol

Place a strip of tape around the inside rim of the bowl to serve as a guide for painting the dots. Use the marker to draw the dots, widely spaced, in a regular line just below the edge of the tape. Attach the nozzle onto the paint tube and cover the dots you made with small round dots of paint. Always work in a well-ventilated room.
Fire according to the instructions on page 12, then let the items cool completely. Finish by removing any remaining traces of marker with rubbing alcohol.

Vase cozy

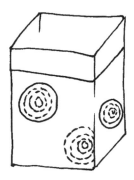

Materials
Square glass vase
Unbleached linen or cotton fabric
Cotton embroidery floss (we used navy blue)
Scissors
Embroidery needle and hoop
Straight pins
Tape measure

Measure the height and circumference of the vase, then add ¾ inch (2cm) to each measurement and cut a rectangle of fabric to this size. From the excess fabric, cut out 2 circles in the sizes indicated in the design opposite. Fold over a ⅜-inch (1cm) hem along the top and bottom of the fabric rectangle and iron flat, then sew lines of running stitches along top and bottom using two strands of the embroidery floss.
Pin the fabric circles onto the rectangle, placing them according to the design, and embroider them with a series of concentric circles of running stitches, as shown.
To join the rectangle, fold over a ⅜-inch (1cm) hem of fabric at each end and iron flat. Turn fabric so the right side is on the inside, and sew the seam on the wrong side using running stitches. Turn this fabric sleeve right side out and slip it over your vase.

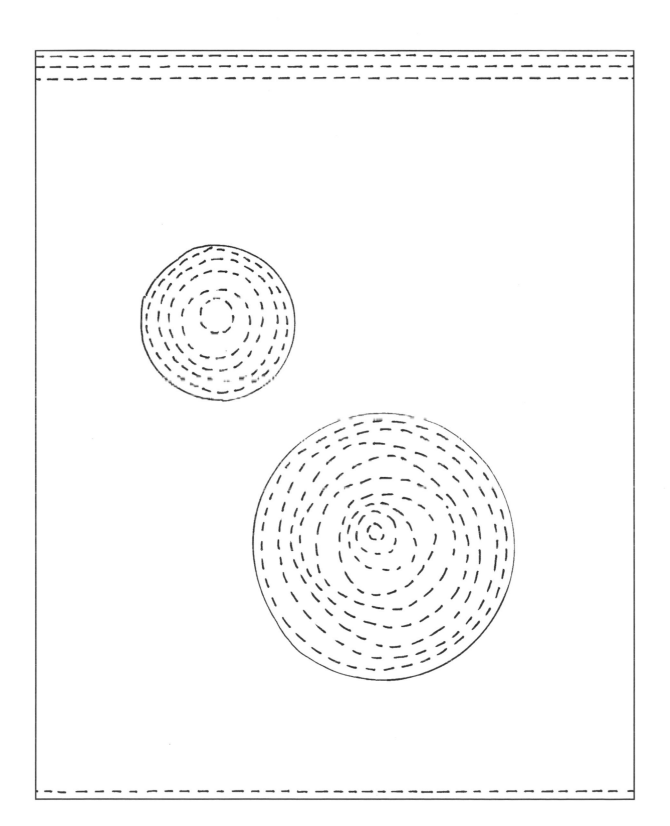

Design shown actual size

Test-tube bud vases

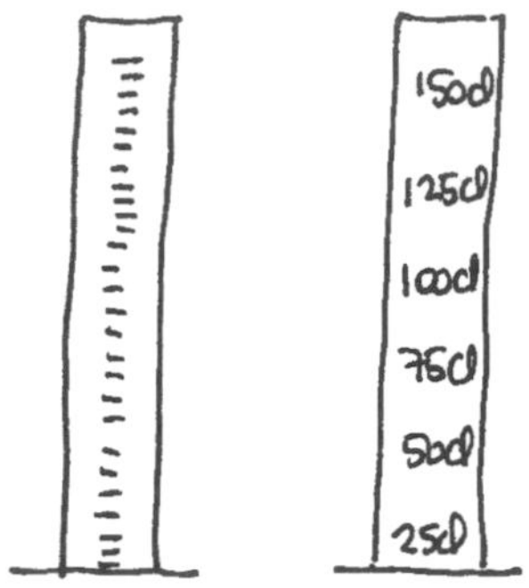

150cl
125cl
100cl
75cl
50cl
25cl

Materials
2 glass laboratory cylinders
Glass engraving tool
Pencil and tracing paper or photocopier
Scissors
Permanent felt-tip marker
Masking tape
Rubbing alcohol
Safety glasses
Dust mask

Use a photocopier or a pencil and tracing paper to copy the designs shown at right. Cut them out, and tape one to the inside of each tube, right side toward the glass. On the outside of the glass trace over the designs with marker, then remove the paper. Engrave the designs wearing safety glasses and a dust mask and following the instructions on page 16. Finish by removing any traces of marker with rubbing alcohol.

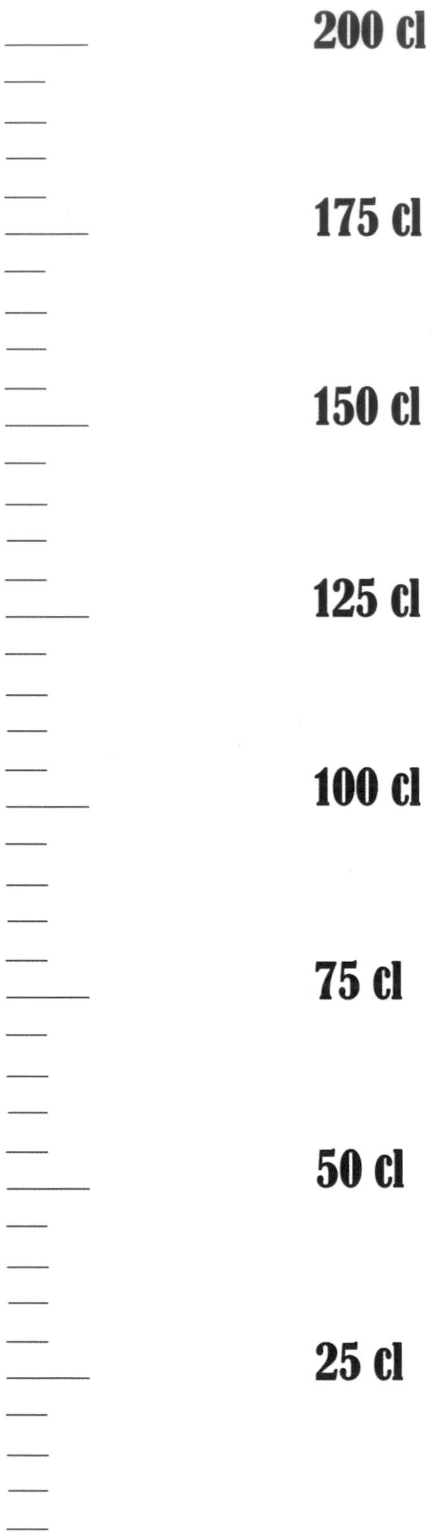

200 cl

175 cl

150 cl

125 cl

100 cl

75 cl

50 cl

25 cl

Designs shown actual size

French pantry jars

Materials
Glass jars
Muslin or other plain cotton fabric
Cotton embroidery floss (we used purple)
Embroidery needle and hoop
Scissors
Tracing paper
Dressmaker's carbon paper
Pencil

Measure the circumference of your jars and add 1 inch (2.5cm). Cut rectangles of fabric this long and approximately 4 inches (10cm) high. Transfer the "Petit Beurre" design below, following the instructions on page 8, and center the design on the fabric rectangles. Use 2 strands of embroidery floss to embroider the design; use blanket stitch for the outline, stem stitch for the words, and French knots for the dots (see pages 8–9 for instructions).
Place the 2 ends of each fabric rectangle together to form a tube and sew them together using blanket stitch. Fray the top and bottom edges slightly for a natural look, then slide the cotton covers onto the jars.

Design shown actual size

Autumn plates

Materials
3 white porcelain or ceramic dinner plates
Porcelain paint in 2 colors (we used brown for the trees and violet for the bird)
Fine paint tip or nozzle
Natural turpentine (non-toxic)
Tracing paper
Soft pencil
Permanent felt-tip marker
Rubbing alcohol

Using a photocopier, enlarge the designs shown opposite by 240 percent. Trace Design 1 onto tracing paper with a soft pencil. Turn the tracing paper over and go over the lines again thickly with the pencil. Place the tracing, right side up, on a plate and trace over the lines a third time with the pencil, pressing firmly. Remove the tracing paper and use the marker to trace over the lines on the plate. Repeat with Designs 2 and 3 on the remaining plates.
Fit the fine tip or nozzle to your tube of paint and paint over the marker lines.
When you have painted all the tree designs, clean the nozzle thoroughly with natural turpentine and working in a well-ventilated room. Attach the nozzle to the second color and add the origami bird to the third plate. Allow the plates to dry thoroughly.
Fire the plates, following the directions on page 12. Let cool completely, then remove any traces of marker with rubbing alcohol.

Enlarge designs 240%

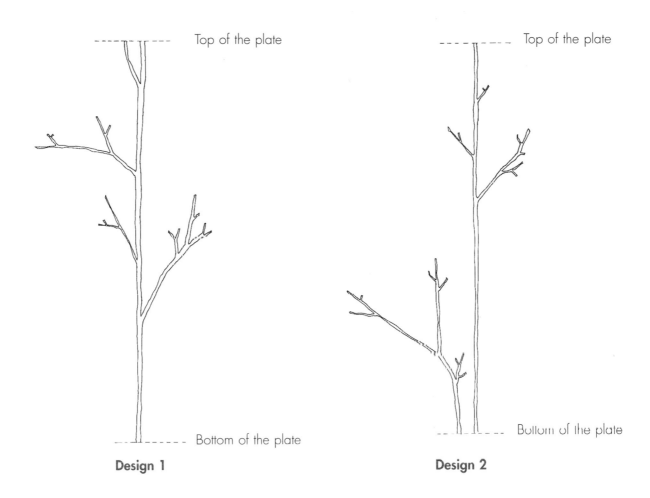

- - - - - - - - Top of the plate

- - - - - - - - Top of the plate

- - - - Bottom of the plate

- - - - Bottom of the plate

Design 1

Design 2

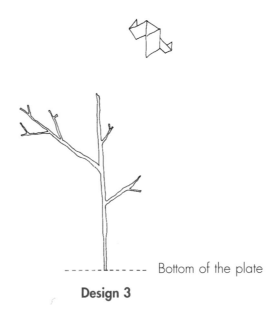

- - - - - - - - Bottom of the plate

Design 3

Dandelion vase

Materials
Round glass vase
Glass engraving tool
Scissors
Permanent felt-tip marker
Masking tape
Rubbing alcohol
Safety glasses
Dust mask

Using a photocopier, enlarge the designs shown opposite by 130 percent or the size that works for the vase you are using. Cut the designs apart and tape them to the inside of the vase, right side toward the glass, positioned as shown on page 30. Trace over the lines with marker, then remove the paper. Engrave the design wearing safety glasses and a dust mask and following the instructions on page 16. Finish by removing any traces of marker with rubbing alcohol.

Enlarge design 130%

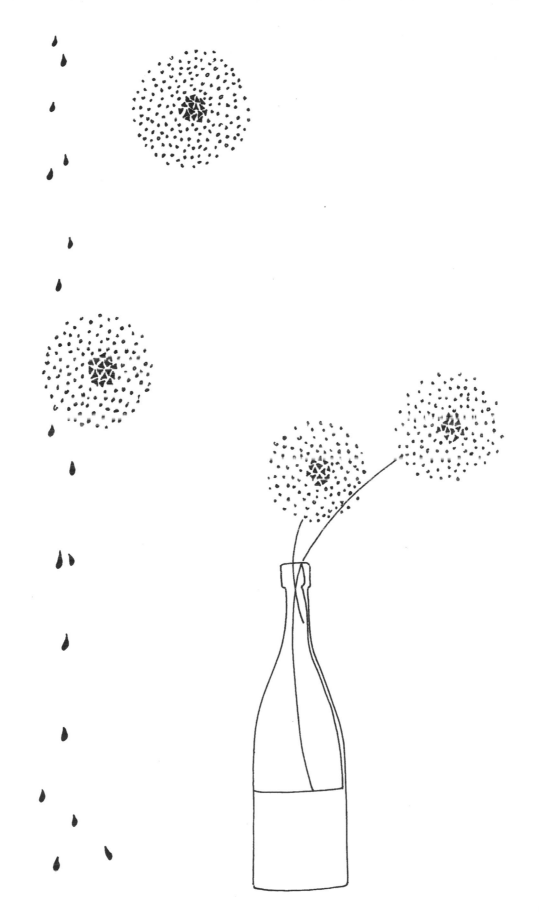

Bouquet vase

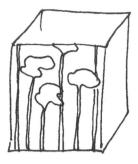

Materials
Square glass vase
Glass engraving tool
Pencil and tracing paper or photocopier
Scissors
Permanent felt-tip marker
Masking tape
Rubbing alcohol
Safety glasses
Dust mask

If necessary, use a photocopier to enlarge the design shown opposite, top, to fit the vase you are using. Cut out the design and tape it to the inside of the vase, right side toward the glass. Trace over the lines with marker, then remove the paper. Engrave the design wearing safety glasses and a dust mask and following the instructions on page 16. Finish by removing any traces of marker with rubbing alcohol.

Clover glasses

Materials
3 tall glasses
Glass engraving tool
Scissors
Permanent felt-tip marker
Masking tape
Rubbing alcohol
Safety glasses
Dust mask

Using a photocopier, enlarge the designs shown opposite, bottom, by 160 percent. Cut them apart and tape one to the inside of each glass. Trace over the lines with marker and remove the paper. Engrave the designs wearing safety glasses and a dust mask and following the instructions on page 16. Finish by removing any traces of marker with rubbing alcohol.

Design shown
actual size

Enlarge designs 160%

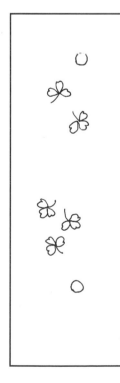
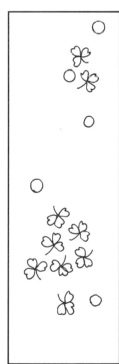

chine

stella

Pot de ......

Blankets,
sheets,
towels…
and other
household
linens

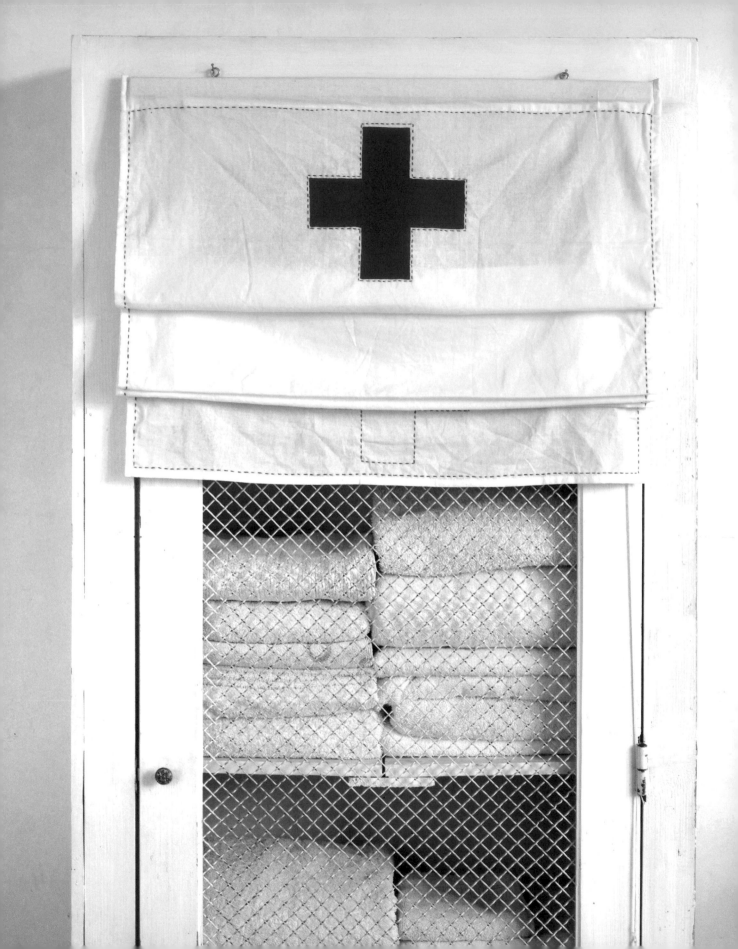

First aid cabinet cover
Instructions on page 70

Snuggly throw
Instructions on page 71

Springtime pillows

Instructions on pages 72–75

Bubble bath towels

Instructions on page 76

"33" blanket

Instructions on page 77

Circle curtains
Instructions on pages 78–79

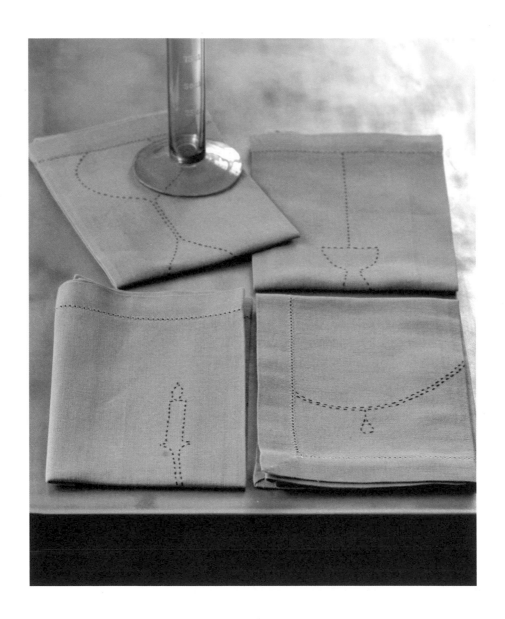

Striped bed set
Instructions on pages 84–85

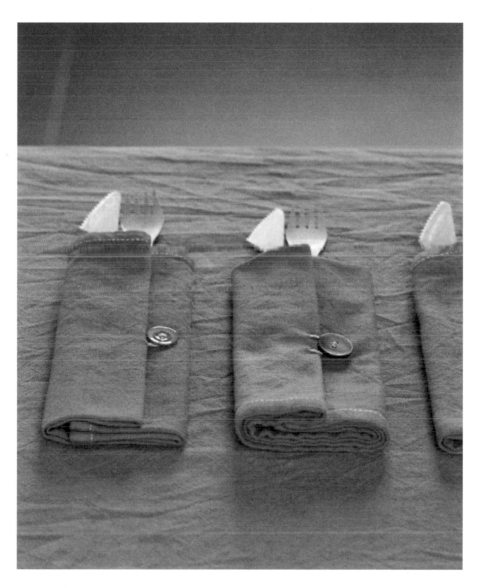

Button napkins
Instructions on page 84

Slipcovers
Instructions on pages 86–89

Clothesline bed cover

Instructions on pages 90–91

Wash-up dishtowels

Instructions on page 92

Un, deux, trois bed set

Instructions on page 93

First aid cabinet cover

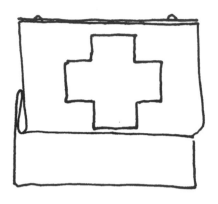

Materials
Roman shade in a cotton fabric
Tracing paper
Dressmaker's carbon paper
Pencil
Red fabric paint
Large paintbrush
Red cotton embroidery floss
Embroidery needle and hoop
Scissors
Iron

Use a photocopier to enlarge the design below by 150 percent. Then trace it onto the cotton shade following the instructions on page 8. Use fabric paint and a paintbrush to paint the cross red. Let dry. Place a sheet of paper over the painted design and press for 5 minutes with a hot, dry iron to set the paint. To finish, use 2 strands of embroidery floss to sew an outline all around the cross, ⅛ inch (3mm) out from the edge, in running stitch. If you like, make another cross at the bottom of the shade, outlining it in running stitch only. Finish with a line of running stitches all around the blind, ⅜ inch (1cm) in from the edge.

Enlarge design 150%

Snuggly throw

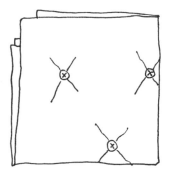

Materials
Cotton fabric, 50 x 30 inches (125 x 75cm)
Terrycloth fabric or a towel, same size and color
Thick polyester or polyester/cotton quilt batting,
about 49 x 28 inches (120 x 70cm)
8 pearl buttons
Thread to match fabric
Sewing needle
Scissors
Safety or straight pins
Sewing machine

Place the cotton and terrycloth fabric pieces right sides together and machine stitch around the edges, leaving an 8 inch (20 cm) opening at one end. Turn right side out. Insert the quilt batting into this cover, and sew the opening closed by hand, using small stitches. Following the diagram below, mark the places for the buttons with pins. Sew a pearl button firmly at each mark, sewing through all 3 layers of fabric.

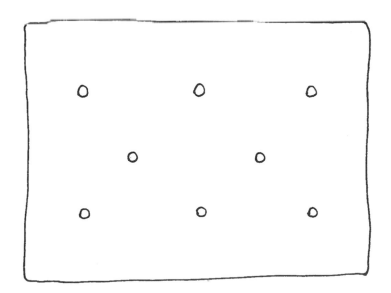

Diagram for button placement

Springtime pillows

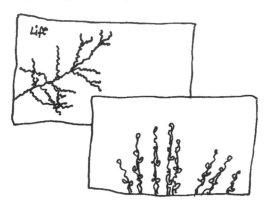

Materials
2 plain pillows, each 28 x 14 inches (70 x 33cm)
Fabric paint in two colors (we used brown and olive green)
Fine paintbrush
Letter stamps (optional)
Tracing paper
Dressmaker's carbon paper
Pencil
Iron

Use a photocopier to enlarge the design opposite by 500 percent, and the design on pages 74–75 by 270 percent. Transfer each design onto a pillow, following the instructions on page 8. Paint the designs with a fine paintbrush, one in each color.

Add the word "life" (or any word you like) to one pillow as shown, using letter stamps dipped in fabric paint. You can do all the letters in one color, or alternate the colors. Let dry, then place a clean cloth over the designs and set them by carefully pressing with a hot, dry iron for 5 minutes.

Enlarge design 500%

life

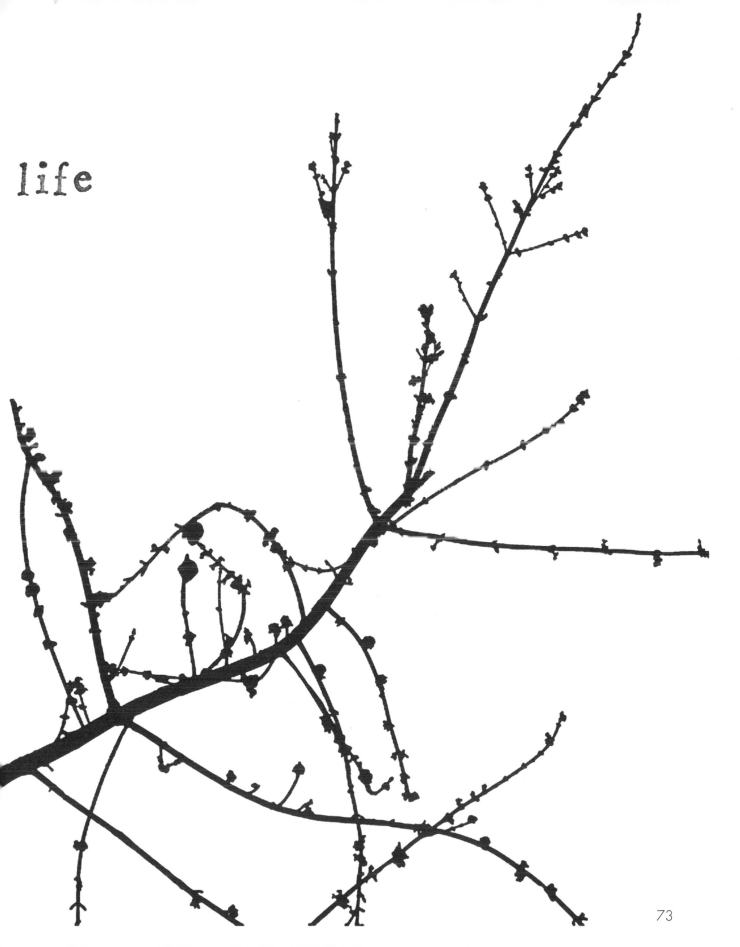

Enlarge design 270%

Bubble bath towels

Materials
2 bath towels
Remnants of printed fabric
Cotton embroidery floss in colors to match fabric
Sewing thread to match towels
Sewing and embroidery needles
Scissors
Straight pins

For the towel with "bubbles," cut circles from the printed fabric, tracing around 2 or 3 small glasses of different sizes, or using the pattern below. Fold under a small hem around the edge of each circle, trimming the fabric as necessary, and iron flat. Arrange the circles on the towel as shown in the diagram below and pin in place. Sew them to the towel by hand, using small running stitches.
Using 2 strands of embroidery floss, sew a line of running stitches across the width of the towel, ¾ inch (2cm) up from the edge.
For the second towel, cut a strip of fabric 2 inches (5cm) high and the width of the towel. Turn under a ³⁄₁₆-inch (0.5-cm) hem all around and iron flat. Pin the strip to the towel, ¾ inch (2cm) up from the edge. Sew the strip to the towel by hand, using small running stitches.

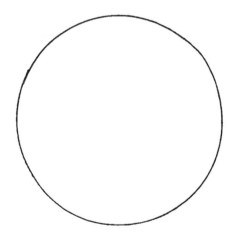
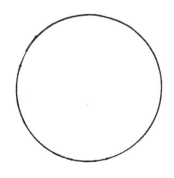
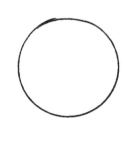

Design shown actual size

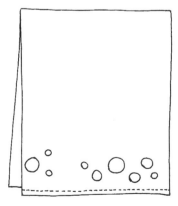

Diagram for circle placement

76

"33" blanket

Materials
Solid color wool blanket
Cotton embroidery floss (we used purple)
Embroidery needle and hoop
Scissors
Tracing paper
Dressmaker's carbon paper
Pencil

Use a photocopier to enlarge the "33" design below by 200 percent, then transfer it to one corner of the blanket, following the instructions on page 8. Embroider the outline of the numbers in fairly long running stitches, approximately 2 stitches every ¾ inch (2cm), using 2 strands of embroidery floss. Below the numbers, embroider 2 lines of running stitches the entire length of the blanket, 1½ inches (4cm) apart.

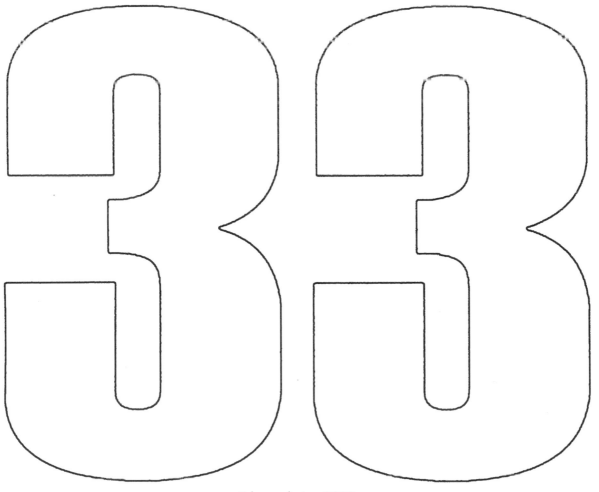

Enlarge design 200%

Circle curtains

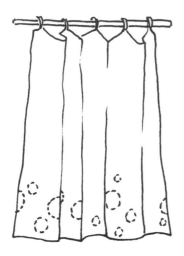

Materials
Lightweight white cotton curtain panels
Cotton embroidery floss (we used chocolate brown)
Embroidery needle and hoop
Scissors
Tracing paper
Thin cardboard
Pencil
Vanishing fabric pen or pencil (see note below)

Use a photocopier to enlarge the circles opposite by 120 percent. Transfer them to the cardboard, then cut out the cardboard circles to use as templates. Draw around the circle templates with a vanishing fabric pen on the lower part of the curtain, following the diagram below, to create the design. Using 2 strands of embroidery floss and a running stitch, embroider the outlines of the circles. The marks of the fabric pen will disappear after a few days.

Note: There are 3 types of fabric markers. Vanishing markers have ink that will disappear in time, washable markers have ink that will wash out with water, and permanent markers are like fabric paint and will remain on the fabric through numerous washings.

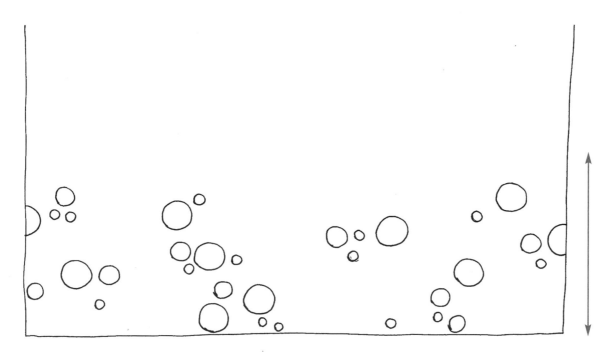

Embroider the bottom 28 inches (70cm) of the curtain.

Diagram for placing the circles

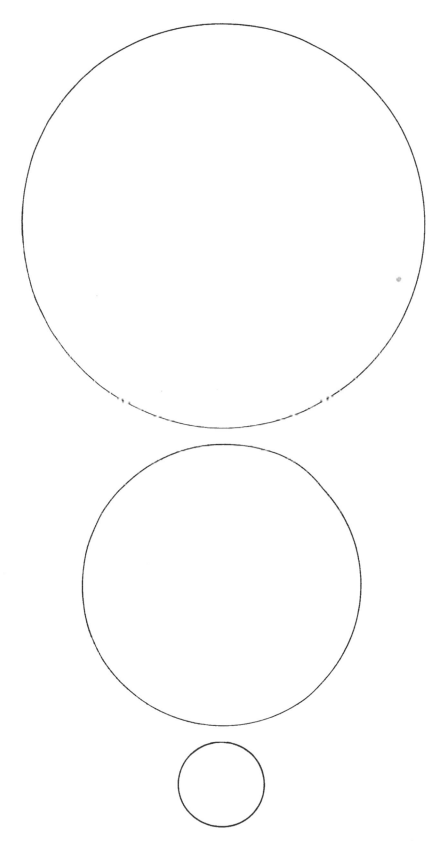

Enlarge designs 120%

Chandelier tablecloth and napkins

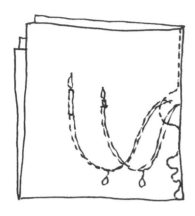

Materials
Linen tablecloth and 4 napkins
Cotton embroidery floss (we used black)
Embroidery needle and hoop
Scissors
Tracing paper
Pencil

Trace Designs 1–4, shown here and opposite, and transfer them to the 4 napkins, following the instructions on page 8. Using a photocopier, enlarge the design on pages 82–83 by 120 percent and, following the instructions on page 8, transfer it to the center of the tablecloth. Using 2 strands of embroidery floss, embroider the outline of each design in running stitch.

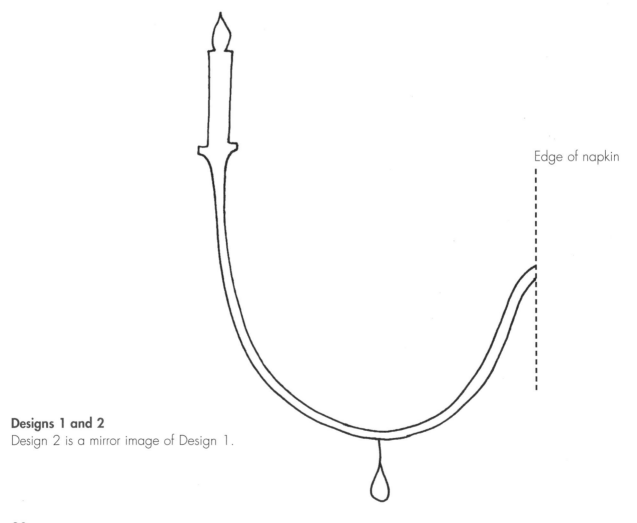

Edge of napkin

Designs 1 and 2
Design 2 is a mirror image of Design 1.

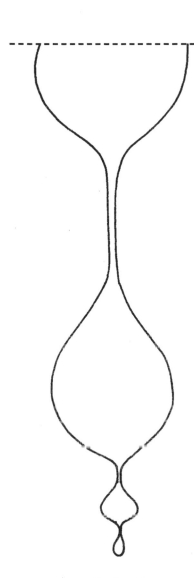

- - - Edge of napkin

Design 3

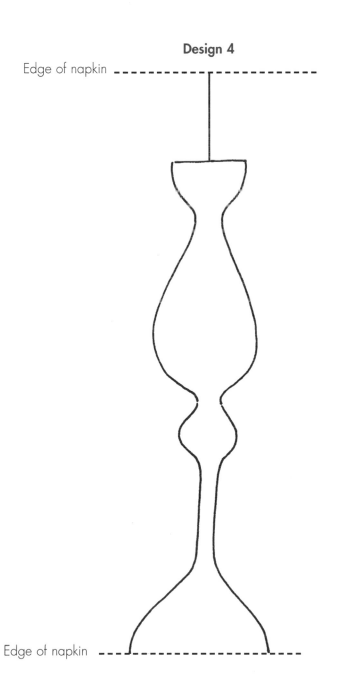

Design 4

Edge of napkin - - - - - - - - -

Designs shown actual size

Edge of napkin - - - - - - - - -

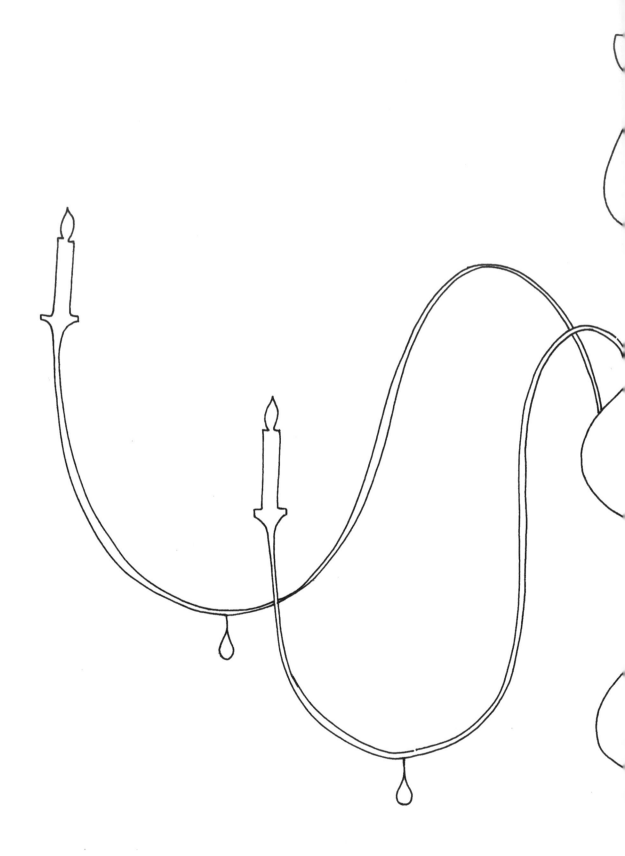

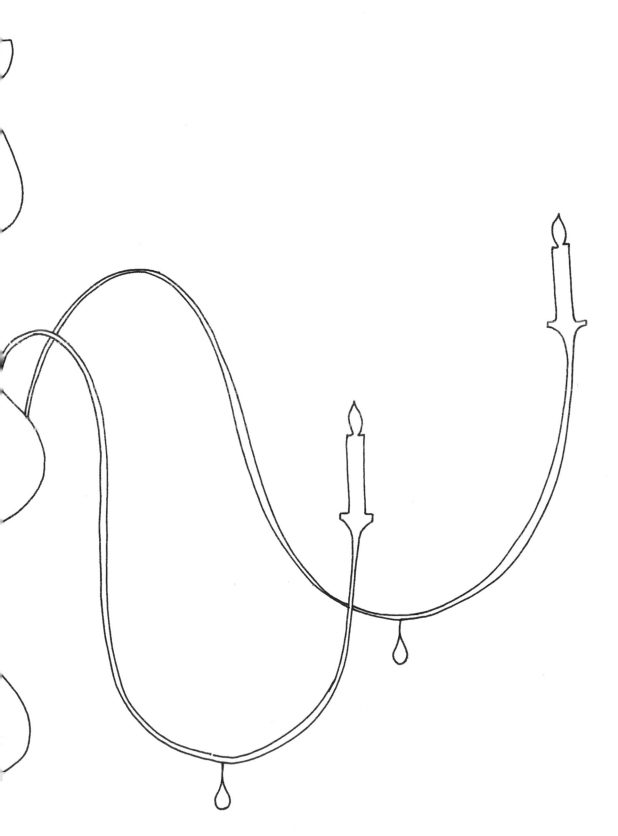

Enlarge design 120%

Striped bed set

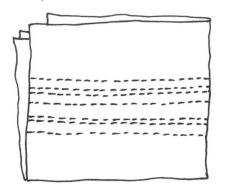

Materials
White cotton queen-size duvet cover or top sheet
2 white cotton pillowcases or pillow shams
Cotton embroidery floss in 3 colors (we used khaki,
plum, and gray)
Embroidery needle and hoop
Scissors
Vanishing fabric pen (see note on page 78)

Following the diagrams opposite, draw lines across the width of the duvet cover or top sheet and pillowcases with a vanishing fabric pen. Using 2 strands of embroidery floss, embroider the lines in running stitch, alternating the colors as indicated. The fabric pen lines will disappear after a few days.

Button napkins

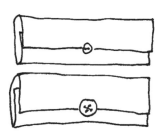

Materials
Cotton napkins
Machine fabric dye (optional; we used taupe)
Cotton embroidery floss (we used pale pink)
Odd pearl buttons in different sizes

If the napkins are new, wash them first; if they have already been washed, simply wet them. Dye them with the taupe dye, following manufacturer's instructions and the tips on page 10. Lay flat to dry.
Using 2 strands of embroidery floss, outline the hem of the napkin along all 4 sides with a running stitch, and sew a button in the center of one side of each napkin, 1½ inches (4cm) from the edge.
To make a loop closure, braid 3 double-strands of embroidery floss. Sew the ends of the braid on the wrong side at the center of the side of the napkin opposite the button, 1½ inches (4cm) from the edge. The loop should be long enough to fasten the button when the napkin is rolled up.

khaki — – – — – — — — – — – — –
plum ▬ – ▬ – – – – – — – ▬

Begin embroidery 20 inches (50cm) from top edge

Duvet cover or top sheet

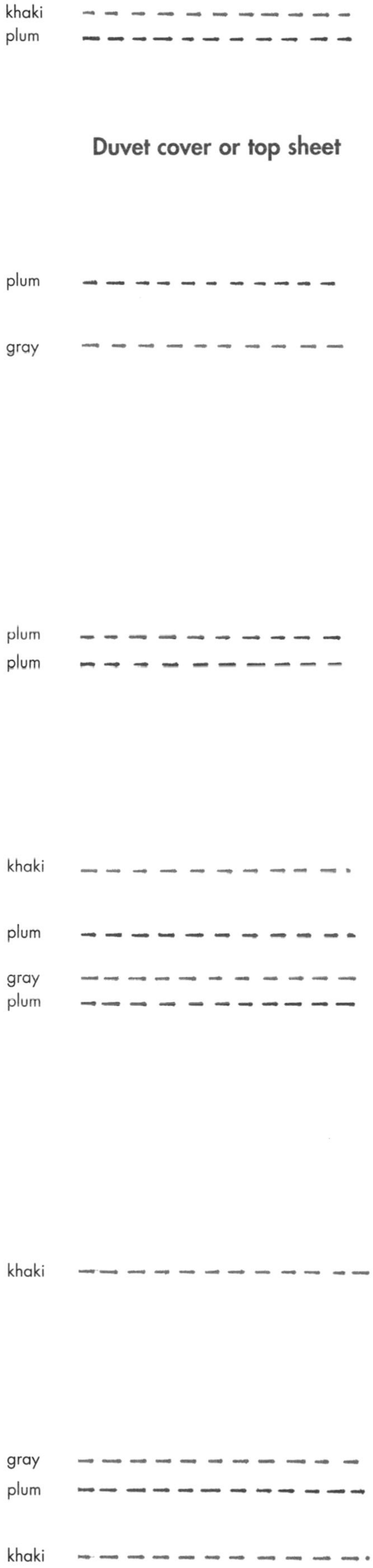

Begin embroidery 8 inches (20cm) from top edge

plum — – — – – – — — – —

khaki — – — — — – — — — — —
plum ▬ – – — – — — – — – —

gray — – — — – — — – —

Pillowcases

plum — – — – — — – — —

gray — – — – — – — — — —
plum ▬ — — – — – — — — ——

plum — – – — — – — — —
plum — – – — – — — — —

khaki — – — – — — — — —

khaki — — — — – — – — — — ▬

plum — – — — – — — — —

gray — — — — – — – — — — —
plum — – — – — – — — — —

gray — — — — – — — — — —
plum — — — — – — — — — ——

khaki — — — — — — — — — —

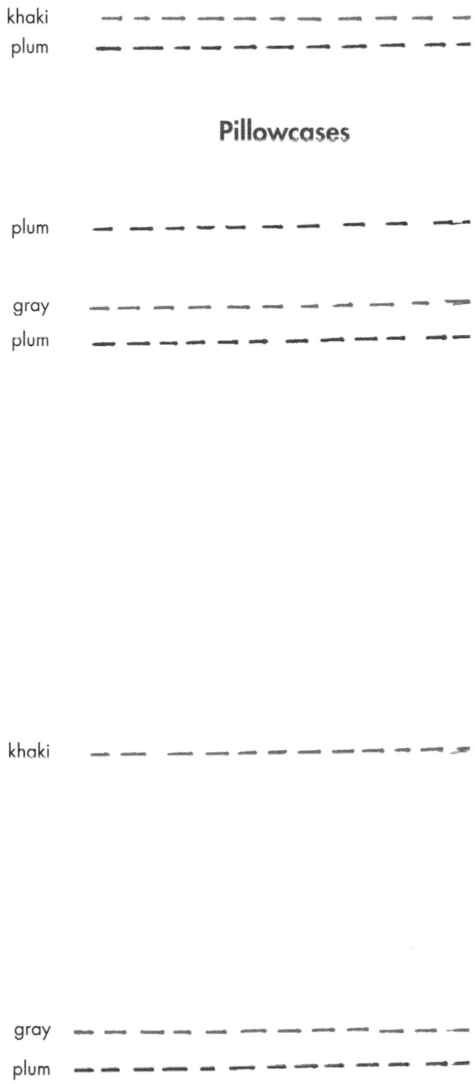

Diagrams for stitching

gray — – — — – — — — —
plum — – — — – — — — — —

khaki — – — — — — — — — .

Slipcovers

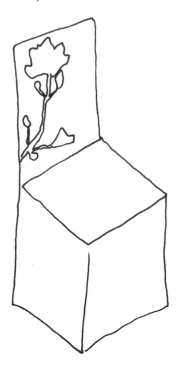

Materials
Cotton slipcovers
Machine fabric dye (optional; we used olive green)
Fabric paint (we used dark green)
Paintbrush
Tracing paper
Dressmaker's carbon paper
Pencil
Clean cloth
Iron

Wash the covers to remove any sizing then dye them in the washing machine, following manufacturer's instructions and the tips on page 10. Allow them to dry thoroughly.
Using a photocopier, enlarge the design opposite by 160 percent and trace onto tracing paper.
Then trace the design on pages 88–89 at same size. Following the instructions on page 8, transfer the designs to the slipcovers, positioning them on the fronts of the chair backs as shown on pages 64–65. Put the covers on the chairs so the fabric is stretched taut and paint the designs with a fine brush. Let dry, then remove the slipcovers from the chairs. Place a clean cloth over the design and press carefully with a hot, dry iron for 5 minutes to set the paint.

Enlarge design 160%

Design shown actual size

Clothesline bed cover

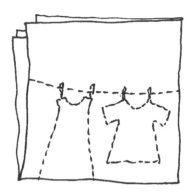

Materials
Twin size cotton duvet cover or top sheet
Cotton embroidery floss (we used navy blue)
Embroidery needle and hoop
Scissors
Dressmaker's carbon paper
Pencil

Using a photocopier, enlarge the design below by 500 percent. Trace it with a pencil and, following the instructions on page 8, transfer it across the duvet cover or top sheet. Using 2 strands of embroidery floss, embroider the outlines of the design in running stitch.

Enlarge design 500%

Wash-up dishtowels

Materials
2 waffle weave dishtowels
Cotton embroidery floss (we used blue)
Embroidery needle and hoop
Scissors
Fabric paint (we used gray)
Letter stamps
Tracing paper
Dressmaker's carbon paper
Old plate for paint
Clean cloth
Iron

For the embroidered dishtowel, enlarge the washing symbols below by 120 percent, then trace with a pencil and, following the instructions on page 8, transfer onto the center one of the dishtowels.
Using 2 strands of embroidery floss, embroider the outlines of the symbols in stem stitch.
For the other dishtowel, spread fabric paint on an old plate and dip the letter stamps into it, being careful to wipe off any excess paint. Apply the stamps to the dishtowel to spell the suggested phrase, or whatever words you prefer. Allow it to dry thoroughly, then cover the design with a clean cloth and press carefully with a hot, dry iron for 5 minutes to set the paint.
Finish the dishtowels by embroidering a border of running stitch all around, 2 inches (5cm) in from the edge.

Enlarge designs 120%

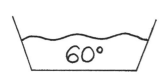  

machine wash. 100% cotton Pure

Phrase for stamping

Un, deux, trois bed set

Materials
Twin size cotton duvet cover or top sheet
Matching cotton pillowcase
Letter stamps
Fabric paint (we used chocolate brown)
Cotton embroidery floss to match fabric paint
Embroidery needle and hoop
Scissors
Tracing paper
Dressmaker's carbon paper
Pencil
Old plate for paint
Clean cloth
Iron

Lay the duvet cover or top sheet flat and trace a line along the length, 20 Inches (50 cm) in from the edge. Pour a little fabric paint onto an old plate. Dip the stamps into it, taking care to wipe off any excess paint, and apply them to the cover. Spell out a list of numbers in ascending order, "un deux trois quatre cinq six" in French, English, or any language—or place the words at random. Create a matching border along one edge of the pillowcase. Allow them to dry completely, then cover the design area with a clean cloth and press carefully with a hot, dry iron for 5 minutes to set the paint.
Use a photocopier to enlarge the number design below by 150 percent, then trace it in pencil and, following the instructions on page 8, transfer it to the cover, centering it 24 inches (60cm) down from the top edge. Using 2 strands of embroidery floss, embroider the outlines of the numbers in running stitch.

Enlarge design 150%

100% coton Pure

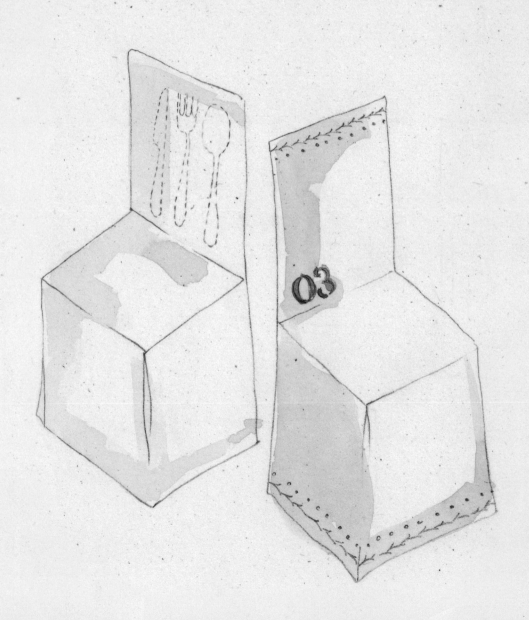

03

Boxes,
buckets,
chests...
and other
containers

Little frames
Instructions on page 108

Medicine cabinet
Instructions on pages 112–113

Provençal herb pots
Instructions on page 112

Zinc storage tub
Instructions on page 114

Wordy flowerpots
Instructions on page 115

Farmhouse chairs

Instructions on page 116

Wall montage
Instructions on pages 117–119

Writer's organizer
Instructions on pages 116–117

Little frames

Materials
Small picture frames of various sizes with mats
Pieces of wallpaper or wrapping paper
Scissors
Spray adhesive
Dust mask

Use frames of different overall size but with the same or similar frame width. Choose wallpaper or sheets of wrapping paper with a historical motif or a design of animals or flowers.

Cut a rectangle of paper to fit inside each frame and glue it to the cardboard backing of the frame, making sure to smooth the paper carefully to avoid creasing it. Wear a dust mask when you use spray adhesive.

Hang the frames on the wall, lining them up on one side, either horizontally or vertically, leaving the same distance between them to create a sense of harmony.

Stamped mini chest

Materials
Small wooden chest of drawers
Wallpaper
Spray adhesive
Acrylic paint
Fine paintbrush
Tracing paper and carbon paper
Pencil
Masking tape
Clear matte acrylic spray varnish
Dust mask

Using a photocopier, enlarge the design on pages 110–111 by 105 percent, then trace it with a pencil and transfer it to the front of the small chest, following the instructions on page 13. Or you could create a design directly on the drawers using purchased stencils.

Tape the drawers shut with masking tape to prevent them from moving, then paint the letters using acrylic paint. Allow them to dry thoroughly.

Measure the depth of the chest and then the height of the two sides plus the width of the top, and cut a rectangle of wallpaper to these dimensions. Lay the paper flat, right side down, and spray with the adhesive. Beginning at the base of one side, attach the paper to the chest, aligning the paper with the front edge of the chest and smoothing it carefully across the top and down the other side. Press firmly, making sure the edges and corners are aligned. Remove the tape holding the drawers in place.

If you like, spray the front of the chest with clear varnish, wearing a dust mask and working in a well ventilated room.

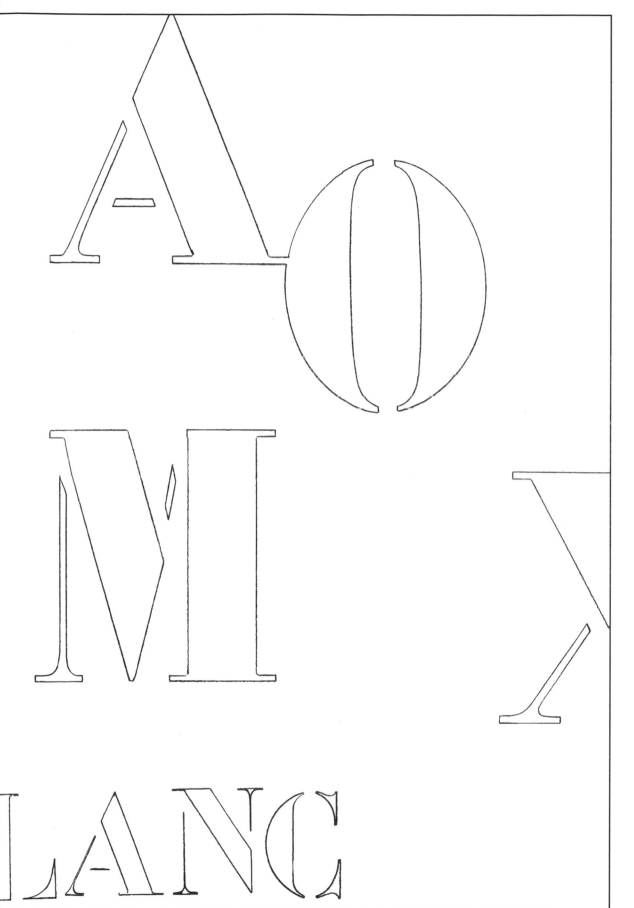

Medicine cabinet

Materials
Metal medicine cabinet
Marbleized or other decorative paper
Thin silk ribbon (we used dark green)
Cotton embroidery floss (we used dark green)
Tracing paper
Embroidery needle
Scissors
Spray adhesive
Dust mask

Using a photocopier, enlarge the cross opposite by 200 percent and transfer it to the decorative paper using the method on page 13. Cut it out, spray the back with adhesive, wearing a dust mask, and attach it to the center of the cabinet door. Cut 1 piece of ribbon the length of the bottom of the cross, and another the width of the cabinet plus the depth of the door. Glue the first piece along the base of the cross and the second across the door about 1 inch (2.5cm) from the bottom edge.
To make the tassel, cut 20 pieces of embroidery floss, each 7 inches (18cm) long, and fold them in half. Slip another piece of embroidery floss through the fold and knot it tightly to hold the strands together, leaving the ends long enough to attach the tassel to the key. Take another piece of floss and wind it tightly several times around the threads below the fold, knot it, then use a needle to poke the knot and tail into the bulk of the tassel. Trim the ends of the strands neatly. Tie the tassel to the key and add a ribbon tie as well.

Provençal herb pots

Materials
3 zinc or galvanized metal pots and 1 container to hold them
Letter stencils (see pages 14–15)
Masking tape
Acrylic paint (we used green)
Stencil brush
Old plate for paint
Clear matte acrylic spray varnish
Dust mask

Divide the letter stencils of the word "herbe" or any word you like between the 3 pots and secure them with tape. Pour a little paint onto the plate and dip the brush into it, taking care to wipe off any excess paint, then apply to the stencils in small dabbing motions. Use the same paint and brush to paint a line around the top of the container on the outside edge. When the paint is dry, spray with clear varnish, wearing a dust mask and working in a well ventilated room. Allow the pots to dry thoroughly.

Enlarge design 200%

Zinc storage tub

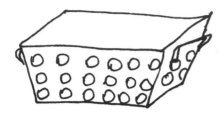

Materials
Zinc or galvanized metal tub
Acrylic paint in 2 colors (we used black and white)
Old plate for paint
Wooden spoon
Flat sponge
Clear matte acrylic spray varnish
Dust mask

Put some paint on a large plate, one color on each side. In the center of the plate, mix a little of the two colors together with the handle of the wooden spoon to get various intermediary shades (we created shades of gray).
To make the stamps, cut the sponge into as many small circles as you have shades of color.
Stamp rows of circles on the outside of the tub, using all the various shades of color. Let dry the paint thoroughly, then spray with matte varnish, working in a well ventilated room and wearing a dust mask.

Wordy flowerpots

Materials
Different sized zinc or galvanized metal flowerpots
Acrylic paint in 2 colors (we used mauve for the base
and black for the words)
Letter stamps
Masking tape
Large paintbrush
Old plate for paint
Clear matte acrylic spray varnish
Dust mask

Use masking tape to mark the borders of the sections to be painted, then paint the pots and allow them to dry thoroughly.
Pour a little black paint onto the plate and dip the stamps into it, making sure to wipe off any excess paint. Press the stamps to the pots gently to form words or names. Let dry thoroughly, then spray with clear varnish, wearing a dust mask and working in a well ventilated room.

(fleurs)

(flowers)

(bloom)

(blume)

(fiore)

Examples of words for stamping

Farmhouse chairs

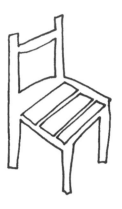

Materials
Small wooden chairs
Acrylic paint in 2 colors (we used green as a base color and navy blue for the letters)
Paint roller
Fine paintbrush
Letter stencils (see pages 14-15)
Masking tape
Stencil brush
Old plate for paint
Clear matte acrylic spray varnish
Dust mask

Paint the chairs in the base color with the roller, using the paintbrush to fill in small areas. Let dry thoroughly. Position the letter stencils on the seat to form a word or name and secure with masking tape. Pour a little of the paint for your letters on the plate and dip the stencil brush into it, being careful to wipe off any excess paint. Apply the paint to the stencils with small dabbing motions. Let dry, then apply a second coat in the same way. Allow them to dry thoroughly before spraying with clear varnish, working in a well ventilated room and wearing a dust mask.

Writer's organizer

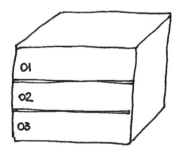

Materials
Small wooden chest with three drawers
Acrylic paint in 3 colors (we used gray, sky blue, and slate blue)
Broad and fine paintbrushes
Old plate for paint
Tracing paper
Soft pencil
Clear matte acrylic spray varnish
Dust mask

Paint the body of the chest and one drawer with the base color (we used gray). Paint the second drawer with the second color (here sky blue) and the third drawer with the third color (here slate blue). Allow the paint to dry thoroughly.
Trace the numbers shown opposite, bottom, and transfer them to the top left corners of the drawers following the directions on page 13. Paint them with the fine paintbrush, using a color that contrasts with the color used on the drawers. Allow to dry thoroughly before spraying with clear varnish in a well ventilated room and wearing a dust mask.

Wall montage

Materials
6 identical wooden picture frames, each 4 x 6 inches (10 x 15cm)
Acrylic paint in 2 colors (we used olive green and purple)
Paintbrush
Clear matte acrylic spray varnish
Dust mask
Ruler
Craft knife or scissors
Masking tape

Paint the frames with the lighter color paint (olive green here) and let dry. On 3 of the frames, draw a line going across the frame at the bottom edge of the photo area. On the other 3, draw a line across the frame measuring down from the top edge a length that is equal to twice the width of the frame. For example, if the frame is 1 inch (2.5cm) wide, you would draw a line 2 inches (5cm) down from the top edge. Mask off these lines with a strip of masking tape and paint the uncovered parts in the darker color (here purple). Let dry, then apply a second coat.

When the frames are completely dry, spray with clear varnish, working in a well ventilated room and wearing a dust mask.

Using a photocopier, enlarge the tree and flower designs on pages 118–119 by 110 percent. Cut them out and put them in the frames.

Hang your frames so the purple stripes align, as shown on page 107.

Enlarge design 120%

Enlarge designs 110%

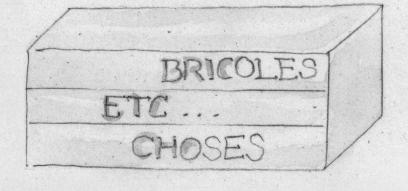

BRICOLES
ETC...
CHOSES

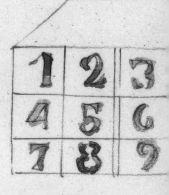

armoire à pharmacie

And still more…

Dyed rug
Instructions on page 132

Le shopping closet boxes
Instructions on page 133

Globe lights
Instructions on page 134

Bon mots painting
Instructions on page 135

Cluster candle trio
Instructions on page 138

Personalized hanger
Instructions on pages 138–139

Dyed rug

Materials
Small wool rug
Cold-water dye (we used a coffee color)
Salt, vinegar or other fixative recommended
by manufacturer
Rubber gloves
Large bucket
Wooden spoon

Put on the rubber gloves. Prepare the dye in a large bucket according to the package directions and the tips on page 10. Wet the rug completely and wring it out just a little before putting it into the bucket of dye. Stir constantly for 5-10 minutes, then at regular intervals for 1 hour, making sure the rug is totally immersed at all times. Work carefully so that you do not breathe in the powdered dye or get the liquid dye in your eyes or on your skin. Do not use dye around small children.

Wring out the rug by hand or spin it in the washing machine on a gentle spin cycle and lay flat to dry, making sure it is not in direct sunlight. Drying it in the sun could fade the color.

Le shopping closet boxes

Materials
Plain cardboard storage boxes with lids
Wallpaper
Craft knife
Spray adhesive
White acrylic paint
Letter stencils (see pages 14–15)
Stencil brush
Masking tape
Old plate for paint
Dust mask

Start by "wrapping" the lids with wallpaper. Cut a rectangle of wallpaper that is longer and wider than the size of the lid. Lay the paper, face down, on a flat surface and spray it with adhesive. Wear a dust mask when you spray. Place the lid in the center of the glued paper and press firmly to make sure the paper sticks to the entire surface. Using a craft knife, make a diagonal cut at each corner and smooth the excess paper up the sides and over to the inside of the lid. Repeat with the second lid.
Choose the letter stencils that spell out whatever you plan to store in the box (or any word you like), and tape them in place on the front of the box. Pour a little white paint onto the plate and dip the stencil brush in, making sure to wipe off any excess paint, and apply to the stencils with light, dabbing motions. Let dry, then apply a second coat the same way.

As a variation (shown on the top box in the photo on page 125), cut out a rectangle of wallpaper for the lid as explained above, but then remove a strip about 4 inches (10cm) wide from the center, leaving two equal rectangles of paper. Apply each piece to the box lid as above, one on each end, leaving a band in the center uncovered. Stencil your initials in the band.

Globe lights

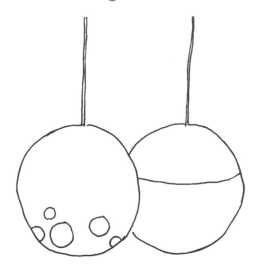

Materials
Collapsible paper hanging globes
For the spotted globe:
    Acrylic paint (we used navy blue)
    Pencil
    Fine paintbrush
    Old plate for paint
For the dyed globe:
    Cold-water dye (we used a coffee color)
    Large bucket
    Wooden spoon
    Rubber gloves

For the spotted globe, pour some acrylic paint onto the plate. Unfold the globe, stretching it over its frame, then delicately draw circles of different sizes on the lower half. Dilute the paint slightly with water and apply it to the circles with a fine brush. Let dry.

For the coffee-colored globe, put on rubber gloves and prepare the dye according to the package directions and the tips on page 10. (See page 132 for safety precautions when working with dye.) Unfold the globe, stretching it over its frame. Hold it at the top and carefully lower it into the bucket of dye to about two-thirds its depth. Let it soak until the paper is thoroughly saturated with the dye. Lift it out and hang it up to dry, placing a pile of newspapers underneath it to catch any drips. Avoid moving the glove until it has dried completely.

Etched mirrors

Materials
2 mirrors, 12 x 12 inches (32 x 32cm)
Tracing paper
Soft pencil
Permanent felt-tip marker
Rubbing alcohol
Glass engraving tool
Safety glasses
Dust mask

Use a pencil and tracing paper and the directions on page 12 to copy the designs on pages 136 and 137. (Enlarge or reduce the designs on a photocopier first if your mirrors are larger or smaller than the ones we used.) Go over the design on the mirror with the marker, being careful not to erase the pencil marks with your hand as you work. Engrave the designs according to the instructions on page 16. Always wear protective glasses and a dust mask when engraving and wipe off any dust carefully as you work. Finish by removing any traces of marker with the rubbing alcohol.

Bon mots painting

la vie est belle

*

Materials
Stretched canvas, 16 x 16 inches (40 x 40cm)
Acrylic paint (we used taupe)
Broad paintbrush
Letter stamps
Black inkpad

Roughly cover the canvas with a coat of the paint, leaving an uneven ⅜-inch (1cm) or so border all around. Let the canvas dry.
Dip the letter stamps into the black ink and write a message across the center of the canvas.
If your stamps don't include an asterisk, paint one with the fine paintbrush.

la   vie est belle

das   leben ist schön

life   is beautiful

la vita e bella

Sample phrases for your canvas

Design shown actual size

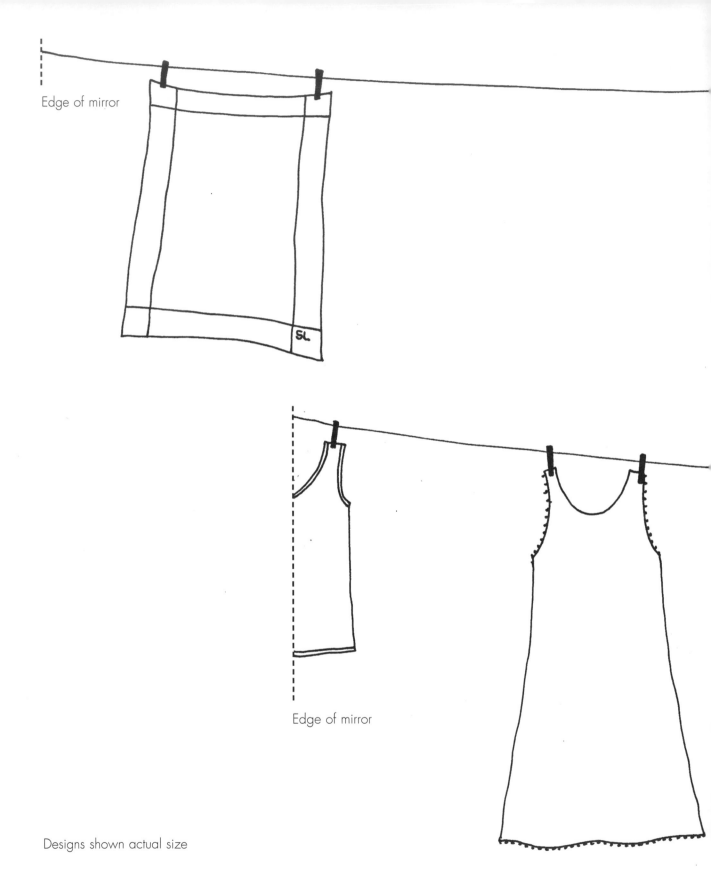

Edge of mirror

Edge of mirror

Designs shown actual size

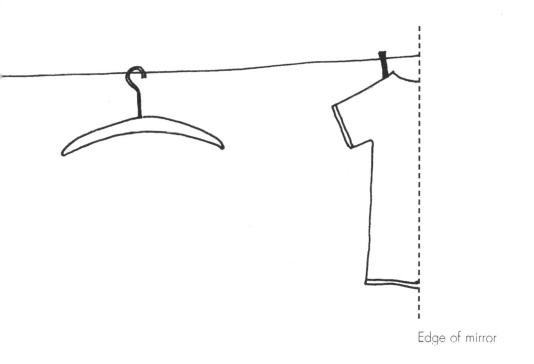

Edge of mirror

I. ♥ NY.

Edge of mirror

137

Cluster candle trio

Materials

1 large candle and 20 slim ones, all the same color
(we used white)
Empty glass jar (an old jelly jar is perfect)
Scrap of unbleached linen or muslin
Cotton embroidery floss (we used chocolate brown)
Embroidery needle and hoop
Star-shaped stamp and brown inkpad
Twigs
Strands of raffia (we used green, natural, and brown)
Transparent or white sewing thread
All-purpose glue

For the jar of candles (far left in the photo), place 8 slim candles in the glass jar (or however many fit in your jar). Cut a 2-inch- (5cm-) wide strip of linen, leaving the edges raw. Using 2 strands of embroidery floss, embroider three parallel lines in running stitch for several inches along the length. Then with the star-shaped stamp and ink, print stars along the length of fabric. Wind the fabric around the pot and secure it with a few stitches.

For the large twig candle (center in photo), glue the twigs all round the candle and finish by tying green raffia around them.

For the candle cluster (shown on the right), use raffia to tie 12 slim candles together in a bundle. Wrap the raffia several times around the candles in the center and then again near the bottom.

Note: These candles are purely for decoration and should *not* be lit.

Personalized hanger

Materials

Wooden clothes hanger
Unbleached linen or muslin
Cotton embroidery floss (we used lime green)
Embroidery needle and hoop
Scissors
Letter stencil (see pages 14–15)
Fabric paint (we used lime green)
Paintbrush
Old plate for paint
Pencil
Masking tape
Straight pins

Fold the linen in half, wrong sides together. Use a photocopier to enlarge the pattern opposite by 110 percent, or just place your hanger on the fabric with the bottom of the hanger along the fold of the fabric and draw around its contours with a pencil. Draw another outline ⅜ inch (1cm) outside the first line and cut out the pattern.

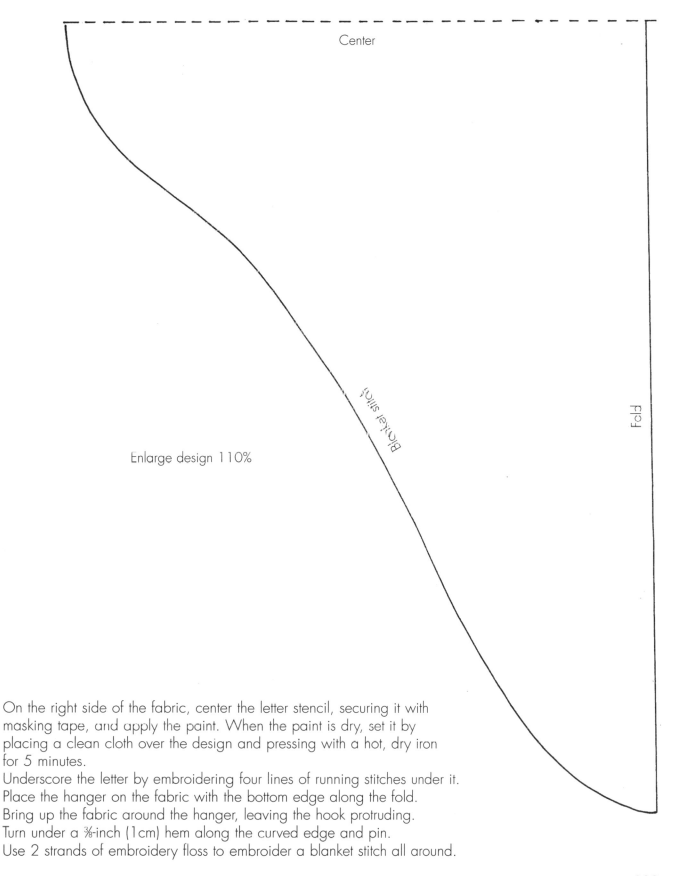

Center

Fold

Blanket stitch

Enlarge design 110%

On the right side of the fabric, center the letter stencil, securing it with masking tape, and apply the paint. When the paint is dry, set it by placing a clean cloth over the design and pressing with a hot, dry iron for 5 minutes.

Underscore the letter by embroidering four lines of running stitches under it.

Place the hanger on the fabric with the bottom edge along the fold.

Bring up the fabric around the hanger, leaving the hook protruding.

Turn under a ⅜-inch (1cm) hem along the curved edge and pin.

Use 2 strands of embroidery floss to embroider a blanket stitch all around.

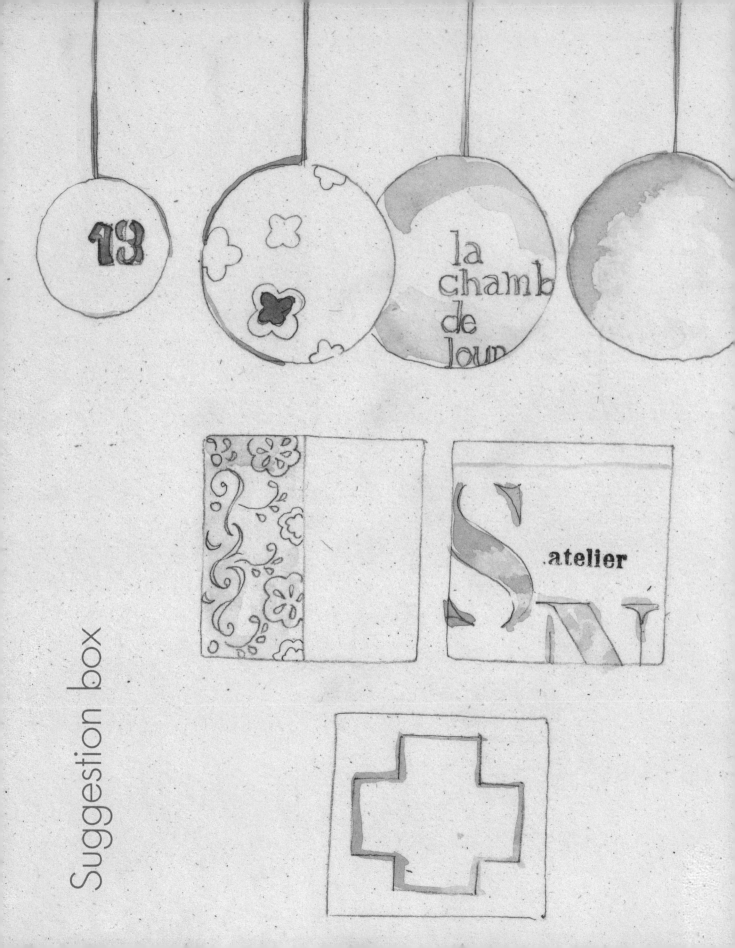

Suggestion box

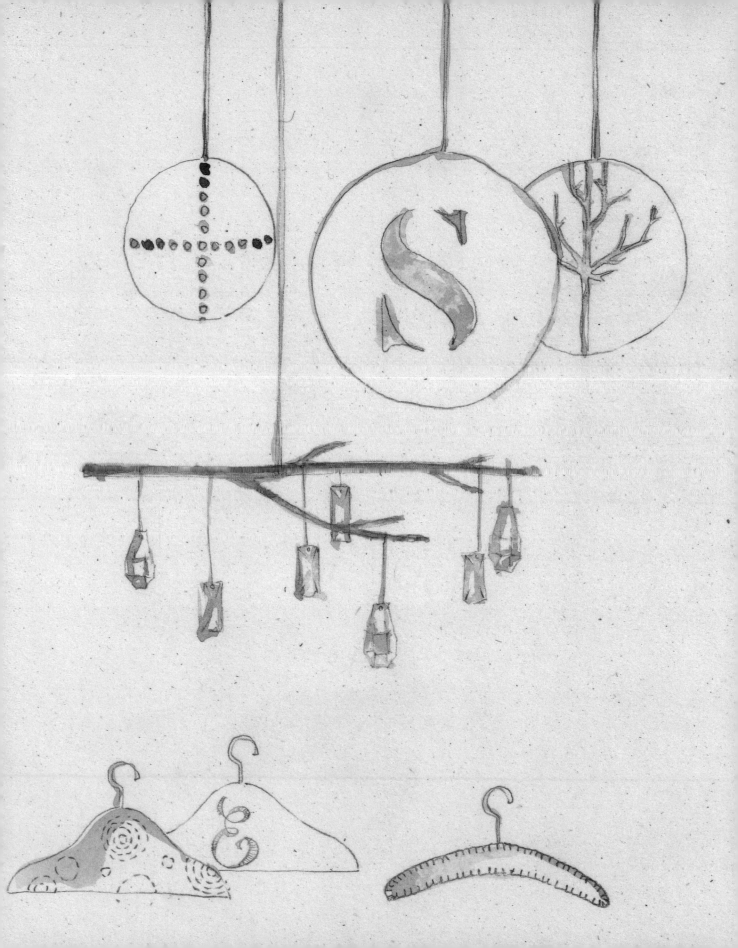

Acknowledgements

Our thanks to Serendipity, who so kindly opened their doors to our photographer and allowed us to use their products:

Velvet Chic (Love pillow), page 53
La Sensitive (silk quilts), pages 57, 102, 105, and 124
Nana ki (cotton quilts), pages 53 and 69
Mushkane (turquoise felt rug), page 27
Talix (stools and metal chairs), pages 56, 59, and 66
Atelier LZC (metal birds), page 54
Tsé-tsé associées (ceramic lamps and vase), pages 128–129
Jielde (vintage lamps), pages 98 and 106

A thousand thanks to Pascale, Laurence and Élisa, Karine and Jérome, Muriel from Loisirs et Création, and Jaqueline from Dylon...and, of course, Dominique and Frédéric.

First published in the United States in 2008 by
Watson-Guptill Publications
Nielsen Business Media, a division of The Nielsen Company
770 Broadway, New York, NY 10003
www.watsonguptill.com

Library of Congress Control Number: 2007936312

ISBN-10: 0-8230-9842-7
ISBN-13: 978-0-8230-9842-2

First published in France by Marabout (Hachette Livre) in 2006
© Marabout 2006

Typeset by Les PAOistes
Printed in Singapore by Tien Wah Press

1 2 3 4 5 6 7 / 14 13 12 11 10 09 08